W9-ARK-235
WOLVES
BY GAIL GIBBONS
Holiday House / New York

For Judie Davie
and Keith Wright

Printed in the United States of America

Library of Congress Cataloging-in-Publication Data
Gibbons, Gail.
Wolves / by Gail Gibbons. — 1st ed.
p. cm.
ISBN 0-8234-1127-3
1. Wolves—Juvenile literature. [1. Wolves.] I. Title.
QL737.C22G52 1994 94-2108 CIP AC
599.74′442—dc20
ISBN 0-8234-1202-4 (pbk.)

ISBN-13: 978-0-8234-1127-6 (hardcover)
ISBN-13: 978-0-8234-1202-0 (paperback)

ISBN-10: 0-8234-1127-3 (hardcover)
ISBN-10: 0-8234-1202-4 (paperback)

The other type of wolf is the red wolf. Red wolves aren't really red. Instead, they are the combination of black, gray and reddish brown. They are smaller and more slender than gray wolves. Only one of the three original different kinds of red wolves exists today. Very few of them live in the wild.

The first ancestors of wolves lived more than 50 million years ago. Over time, these creatures developed into wolves.

It is a snowy moonlit night in the northern woods. An animal shakes the snow from its thick fur, throws its head back and joins its companions in a long howl. The animal is a wolf.

There are two different types of wolves. One is the gray wolf, or timber wolf. A gray wolf can have black, white, brown or gray fur depending on where it lives. Thirty-two different kinds of gray wolves have been identified. Some of them don't exist anymore.

Wolves are members of the dog family called Canidae. All dogs are related to wolves.

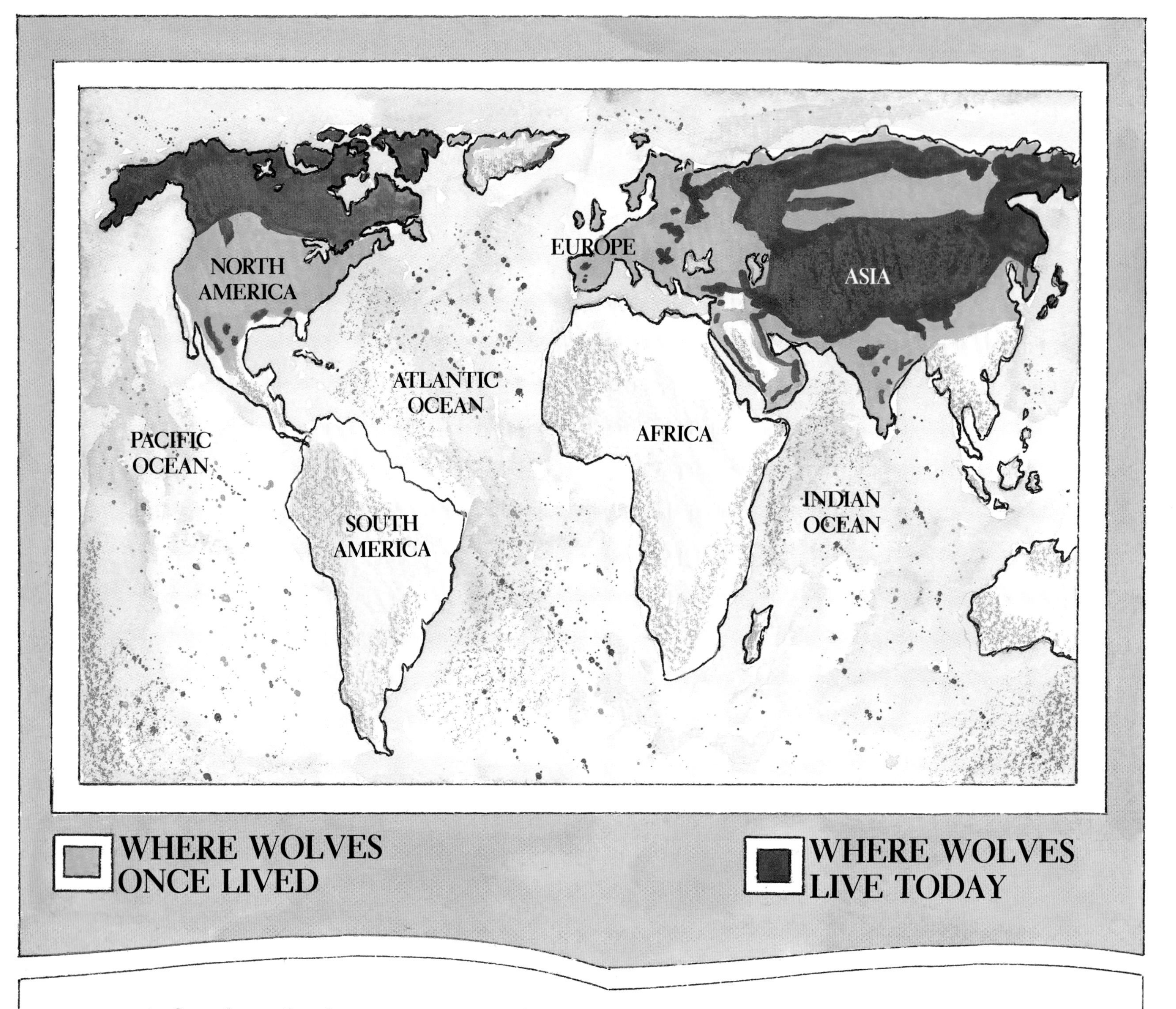

A few hundred years ago, wolves lived all around the world. People hunted them and also took over much of their territory. There were fewer wolves and they moved away. Today most wolves are found in the northern parts of the world.

Most male wolves weigh more than 100 pounds. The females weigh less. Wolves are very strong and have long legs, a long tail, and are covered with fur.

Wolves are hunters. They are carnivores, which means they eat meat. They have strong jaws and forty-two teeth for tearing, chewing and grinding. Four of the teeth are called canine teeth, or fangs. Wolves use their canine teeth to grip an animal when they catch it.

Wolves have a keen sense of smell for sniffing out their prey. They can hear sounds from far away, too. When wolves roam, they leave big paw prints behind. Some tracks can be as large as a grownup's hand.

Gray wolves live in groups called packs. These packs can be made up of three to more than twenty wolves. It is believed that red wolves don't form packs. Wolf packs live and hunt in territories which can cover an area as big as 500 square miles. They mark the boundaries with their urine, which leaves a scent that warns other wolf packs to stay away. Each pack has adult males and females, and their pups.

The leader of a pack is called an alpha wolf. An alpha wolf is smart and strong. It will fight any wolf that tries to take over his pack. The alpha wolf is the tallest in the pack. When he looks the other wolves in the eye, they crouch down and tuck their tails between their hind legs. Sometimes they roll over and lick the alpha wolf's face, letting him know he's boss.

The members of a pack care for each other. They protect each other when other wolf packs try to invade their territory. They hunt and share their food together, too. The alpha wolf decides where and when to hunt. It would be difficult for a wolf to catch a big animal alone. Hunting in packs helps them survive.

Once they spot their prey, the chase begins. Wolves' legs are built for speed and running long distances. Often, an animal outruns them. Other times the prey tires and slows down.

The pack fans out in a circle around the animal. Then one wolf charges and attacks the animal. It hangs on tightly. Others attack.

Soon the fight is over. The hungry wolves can eat. Wolves hunt many different kinds of animals like moose, deer and caribou. They also hunt smaller animals such as rabbits, beavers and small rodents.

Wolves make different sounds to "talk" to each other. They whimper when they are excited or restless. A snarl means the wolf is being threatened. A short woof is a warning, and a bark means danger is near.

Wolves howl, too. The sound is eerie and sometimes seems sad. They howl to tell other packs to stay out of their territory. Often, it is the way they stay in touch with the others in their pack when they are separated. Sometimes they howl before a hunt.

Wolves communicate in other ways, too. They show their teeth when they are angry. When a wolf is scared, its ears go flat against its head. A wagging tail means the wolf is happy. If just the tip of the tail wags, it could be ready to attack.

Wolves often mate for life. Wolf pups are born in the spring. The alpha female is the only one of the females in a pack to give birth to a litter of pups. There can be three to fourteen pups. They only weigh about one pound at birth and cannot see or hear. They nuzzle up against their mother to drink her milk in the den where they live.

When the pups are about three weeks old, they are allowed out of their den to romp and play. The mother and some of the other wolves take turns babysitting while the rest of the pack is hunting. When the hunters return, the pups greet them. When they lick the wolves jaws, the wolves bring up some of the food they have eaten and feed it to the pups. The pups are now old enough to eat meat.

At six months old the pups are almost as big as the adult wolves. They are strong enough and old enough to begin learning how to hunt. They join the pack as it roams in search of food.

For centuries people have been afraid of wolves. They thought wolves were their enemies. Scientists who study wolves are learning that wolves have been misunderstood. Wolves tend to live peacefully among themselves. They are shy and rarely attack people. When this happens, they have probably been threatened.

When wolves hunt, often the animals they kill are weak and sickly. The healthy and stronger animals survive. Wolves are not cruel. They are just very efficient hunters.

Occasionally wolves attack farm or ranch animals. This can make the farmers or ranchers want to kill them. Wolves are hunted for their fur, too.

Because wolves are in danger of extinction, some people realize they must be protected. Some scientists and people who work at zoos help wolves by raising them so they can be released into the wild. In many parts of the world laws have been passed making it illegal to hunt wolves.

By studying wolves in their natural surroundings and watching them for long periods of time, scientists have learned that wolves play an important part in the balance of our natural world. The old fears and myths about wolves are dying. Wolves deserve to live undisturbed.

If enough people care, there will be wild wolves for years to come, and the howling sounds these beautiful creatures make will still be heard.

MORE WAYS OF THE WOLVES

Wolves are the largest of the wild dogs, which include coyotes, foxes and others.

Wolves have very few enemies. These enemies can be other packs of wolves, bears, and people.

Wolves usually trot or run in a way called loping. They are very fast runners. Some can run up to forty miles per hour.

A pack of howling wolves can be heard from as far away as ten miles.

When wolves hunt in snow, they walk in single file. They take turns making tracks for the others to walk in.

Wolves vary in size. The smallest kind in the world is the Arabian wolf. It is only about 32 inches long.

In North America there is no record of a healthy wolf ever attacking a person.

Some experts believe ancient people learned how to hunt by watching packs of wolves hunt.

Wolves are good swimmers but rarely follow prey into water during a chase.

In captivity, wolves have been known to live up to seventeen years. In the wild, life is much harder. Wolves usually live to be only nine to ten years old.

WOLF LEGENDS AND MYTHS

ROMULUS AND REMUS

There is an ancient story that tells about two twin babies who were cared for and raised by a wolf. Romulus and Remus were two famous leaders who founded the city of Rome, Italy, in 753 B.C.

WEREWOLVES

Many years ago, during the Middle Ages, people believed wolves were evil. Stories were told of werewolves, people who turned into wolves after dark. They scared and attacked people. Don't worry . . . there's no such thing as a werewolf!

THE SIOUX MAGICIAN

This is an old Sioux Indian story. A Sioux woman was lost in a snowstorm. A pack of wolves saved her life by bringing her food and letting her sleep in their den. They taught her their secrets. When she returned to her tribe, she taught her people the secrets of the wolves. The woman became a powerful magician.

LITTLE RED RIDING HOOD

This is an old European story about a big, bad wolf. He pretended to be Little Red Riding Hood's grandmother. He dressed up and climbed into her bed. The wolf wanted to eat Little Red Riding Hood and her grandmother, but he was found out and they were saved.